YA
967.57104
F877

D1304144

Wayne State College
Conn Library
Children And Young Adult Materials
Examination Center
1998/99

Crisis in Rwanda

CHARLES FREEMAN

Accelerated Reader
Level 9.1

RSVP
RAINTREE
STECK-VAUGHN
PUBLISHERS
The Steck-Vaughn Company

Austin, Texas

APR 1 8 1999
CONN LIBRARY
Wayne State College
1111 Main Street
Wayne, NE 6878⁻

© **Copyright 1999, text, Steck-Vaughn Company**

All rights reserved. No part of this book may be reproduced or utilized in any form or by any means, electronic or mechanical, including photocopying, recording, or by any information storage and retrieval system, without permission in writing from the Publisher. Inquiries should be addressed to: Copyright Permissions, Steck-Vaughn Company, P.O. Box 26015, Austin, TX 78755.

Published by Raintree Steck-Vaughn Publishers, an imprint of Steck-Vaughn Company

Library of Congress Cataloging-in-Publication Data
Freeman, Charles.
Crisis in Rwanda / Charles Freeman.
    p.   cm.—(New perspectives)
    Includes bibliographical references and index.
    Summary: Relates events in Rwanda after the murder of President Habyarimana including the genocide of the Tutsi, the ill-treatment of refugees, and the eventual reconciliation.
    ISBN 0-8172-5020-4
    1. Rwanda—History—Civil War, 1994—Atrocities.
    2. Genocide—Rwanda—History—20th century.
    3. Rwanda—Ethnic relations.
    4. Tutsi (African people)—Crimes against—Rwanda—History—20th century.
    [1. Rwanda. 2. Genocide. 3. Tutsi (African people).]
    I. Title. II. Series: New Perspectives.
    DT450.435.F74   1998
    967.57104—dc21   97-47645

Printed in Italy. Bound in the United States.
1 2 3 4 5 6 7 8 9 0 03 02 01 00 99

Acknowledgments

The Author would like to acknowledge the help given by staff at the international aid charity Oxfam, especially Anna Coryndon, Paul O'Hagan, Nicola Reindrop, and Andy Bastable, in compiling material for this book.

The Author and Publishers thank the following for their permission to reproduce photographs: Camera Press: cover and pages 12b, 15, 17, 20, 24, 25, 29, 31, 32, 33b, 35, 36, 39, 40b, 46, 47, 51, 55, 59; the Hutchison Library: pages 13, 16; Images of Africa Photobank (David Keith Jones): page 11; Popperfoto: pages 3, 5, 6, 21, 22, 34, 37, 41, 42, 48, 50, 52, 54; Topham Picturepoint: pages 1, 4, 7, 12t, 14, 18, 19, 27, 30, 33t, 38, 40t, 45, 49.

Cover photos: A refugee on her way home to Rwanda, 1996; an exercise session at a Rwandese Patriotic Front training camp

Page 1: A Rwandan government soldier, north-west of Kigali, June 1994

CONTENTS

Who Killed Habyarimana?   4

The Continent of Africa   8

Rwanda: Prelude to Genocide   16

Genocide   25

The Refugees   33

Rwanda and the
International Community   41

Reconciliation and Justice   49

Conclusion   56

Date List   60

Resources   61

Glossary   62

Index   63

On a Red Cross truck:
Refugees separated from
their parents as they made
their way back to Rwanda

WHO KILLED HABYARIMANA?

On Wednesday, April 6, 1994, two African presidents were among the passengers of an airplane approaching the airport of the Rwandan capital, Kigali. They were President Juvenal Habyarimana of the small central African state of Rwanda and President Ntaryamisa of the neighboring country of Burundi. The plane was returning from Dar es-Salaam, the capital of Tanzania, where President Habyarimana had been attending a conference on the future of his country.

Suddenly the plane was attacked by missiles fired at it from Masaka Hill, a piece of high ground on the airport perimeter. They were probably Russian SAM missiles, effective anti-aircraft weapons and relatively easy to buy on the world market. Two of them hit the plane, which exploded and crashed in the grounds of President Habyarimana's own palace. Everyone on board was killed.

Juvenal Habyarimana seized power in Rwanda in 1973. Here he is at a press conference in France, in October 1990.

The issue that President Habyarimana had been discussing in Dar es-Salaam was how the Hutu people, the majority of the population of Rwanda, could share power with the Tutsi people, who formed a minority. The two peoples had lived together for centuries, but there had long been open hostility and much bloodletting between them, and Habyarimana, who was a Hutu, had always been reluctant to admit Tutsis to his government.

Gradually he had been forced by international pressure to do so. At a conference in Arusha in Tanzania in 1993, he had signed an agreement (the Arusha Accords) that he would help reconcile the two peoples and allow the Tutsi full democratic rights and a share in his Hutu government. Some opposition politicians had then been admitted to Habyarimana's government. However, the World Bank and the International Monetary Fund, who said that they would only give the country aid if human rights were respected, were still not satisfied that Habyarimana was committed to change. At Dar es-Salaam they had forced Habyarimana again to agree to share power. It was when he was returning home after this second agreement that his plane was shot down.

Who fired the missiles?

No one has ever discovered who fired the fatal missiles. The Rwandan government claimed that it was the Tutsi, as part of a plan to get rid of all the Hutus, but this seems unlikely. The finger pointed in another direction. Habyarimana's government had secretly been recruiting and training young Hutus in groups known as the Interahamwe ("those who stand together"). These groups were armed and taught that the Tutsi were their enemies. They had already been involved in local killings of Tutsis. It seems clear that it was the Interahamwe and others, mainly from the Presidential Guard, who killed Habyarimana because they believed him to be a traitor.

A government soldier in Kigali checks the identity card of a passerby, following unrest in Rwanda in 1990.

The events of the next few hours bore this out. Even before news of the president's death had been broadcast on the radio, Interahamwe and members of the Presidential Guard were setting up roadblocks in Kigali. All Rwandans carried identity cards stating whether they were Hutu or Tutsi, so it was easy for the soldiers to pick out the Tutsi.

The atmosphere in Kigali

Denis Kanywabahizi, a civil servant at the Ministry of Agriculture, described the tensions that arose immediately after the president's death:

"On the evening of the 6th I had been watching a football match and then went to have a drink with a friend. At about 9:30 a friend gave me the news about the plane crash. I decided to head for home straightaway. Shortly after 9:30, I saw that a roadblock had already gone up near my home. A soldier stopped my car and shouted angrily at me. 'The President is dead and you are in a car? Get out!' I left on foot. I reached the Hotel Chez Lando. There was a vehicle full of soldiers. One soldier told me to get inside. I refused, saying 'When people get into your cars they don't come back.' He hit me with the butt of his rifle; I fell to the ground.
I tried to run. He fired and the bullet hit me in the leg. They put me in their car and broke my glasses. We drove around and around until 2:00 A.M. until they left me on the street near my home...." (Quoted in African Rights, *Rwanda, Death, Despair and Defiance*)

Many were set upon and killed. The soldiers then began rounding up opposition politicians and those who had spoken out for human rights—most of them Hutus who favored reconciliation with the Tutsi. Many of these too were killed, including the Prime Minister, Agatha Uwilingiyamana, who died with ten Belgian soldiers who were protecting her.

In a street in Kigali, six days after the president's death: piles of bodies of victims of the massacre.

It was only the beginning. Within a few days the Tutsi themselves had become the main target, and massacres of Tutsis were spreading throughout the country. It seems that the extermination of the Tutsi had been planned and that the assassination of President Habyarimana had been the signal to begin the killings.

April 10, 1994: When fighting broke out in Kigali, President Habyarimana's family and many Europeans were quickly evacuated.

The killing begins

Who killed Habyarimana? One of President Habyarimana's ministers, Francois Xavier Nsanzuwera, had no doubts:

"As soon as I heard the news I knew instantaneously that the President was murdered by his own entourage. They would rather see the country disintegrate than lose their power and privileges. They killed the President to be able to kill everybody else.... My sense is that President Habyarimana was in favor of killing his political opponents but not the general public, that is women and children.... At an international level he would not be able to explain away wholesale massacres of women and children...but this was the aim of the Hutu fanatics.... They had to kill the President in order to be free to kill everyone else they considered an obstacle...they would rather plunge the country into chaos than see their power and privileges diminish...." (Quoted in African Rights, *Rwanda, Death, Despair and Defiance*)

THE CONTINENT OF AFRICA

Rwanda is one of the smallest countries in Africa. In April–May 1994, Rwandese Patriotic Front troops moved through Rwanda, trying to stop the massacres of the Tutsi. Hutus fled to neighboring countries. (See page 33.)

Three times the size of the United States, Africa is a huge continent with a large and fast-expanding population—more than 700 million people. Its very size means that there is no one Africa. Among its varied environments are deserts, lakes, forests, and vast stretches of open grassland. There are hundreds of different cultures and languages and examples of every possible way of surviving, from hunting animals and gathering plants for food, to keeping cattle, and to farming cash crops for European supermarkets.

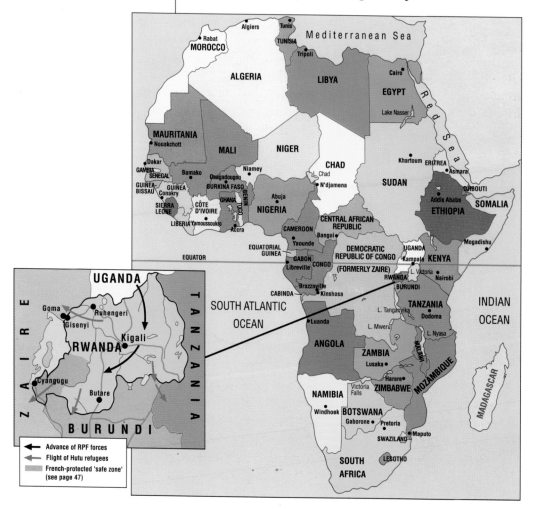

African diversity

Africa is a continent of much diversity, as stressed in this passage from a recent book on African affairs:

"Ways of life, even within the same African country, vary dramatically. Some people may be employed in offices, work in skyscrapers, buy their clothes in department stores, drive cars, and own refrigerators and television sets; others may seldom visit cities, live in rural communities, walk miles in the dry season to fetch water and grow their own food which they cook over wood fires. At the same time, those who live in the cities may have numbers of their extended family with them, seek out traditional healers when they are sick, and participate in centuries-old festivals, while those in rural areas may listen to transistor radios, buy Coca-Cola at local cafes, and welcome a daughter or son back from graduate studies overseas." (Martin and O'Meara, eds., *Africa*)

The majority of Africans work on family farms, producing what they need for themselves, but many drift to the sprawling cities, such as Lagos in Nigeria or Nairobi in Kenya, hoping to find work there. There is so much more to Africa, above all in its color and vitality, than is usually seen on television news or in the press, which tend to focus only on the problems of the continent, its poverty, civil wars, and refugees.

"Compassion without understanding"

An Irish journalist, Fergal Keane, sums up the way in which Africa tends to be seen in the world's media:

"Where television is concerned, African news is generally only big news when it involves lots of dead bodies. The higher the mound, the greater the possibility that the world will, however briefly, send its camera teams and correspondents. Once the story has gone 'stale,' i.e., there are no new bodies and the refugees are down to a trickle, the news circus moves on. The powerful images leave us momentarily horrified but largely ignorant, what somebody memorably described as having 'compassion without understanding.'" (*Season of Blood, A Rwandan Journey*)

Africa also has a rich history. The human race originated on the continent. We are all descended from a small group of humans who crossed into the Middle East some 100,000 years ago. There have been great civilizations on the continent, some well-known, such as that of ancient Egypt, and others that are less well-known in the Western world, such as the medieval kingdoms of Ghana, Mali, and Zimbabwe.

" Village life in northern Ghana

Something of the liveliness of African village life can be gained from this description of a funeral in northern Ghana:

"Dagomba funerals are spectacles. The final funeral of an important or well-loved man or woman can draw several thousand people as participants and spectators. Small-scale traders also come to do business, setting up their tables to sell cigarettes, coffee, tea, bread, fruits, and other commodities to the milling crowds. Spread out over a large area, all types of musical groups form their circles. In several large circles, relatives and friends dance to the music of dondons [drums] and gongons [gongs]. The fiddlers are also there. After a session in the later afternoon people rest and begin reassembling between nine and ten o'clock in the evening. By that time, several groups have already begun playing. After midnight more groups come to dance.... Baamaya dancers dress outlandishly, with bells tied to their feet and waists, wearing headdresses and waving fans. The dance is wonderful and strenuous: while gongons, flutes, and a dondon play the rhythms of Baamaya, the dancers move around their circle, twisting their waists continuously until the funeral closes at dawn." (Chernoff, *African Rhythm and African Sensibility*) **"**

Africa has always been open to outsiders. In the seventh century, Arab conquerors brought the religion of Islam, which spread along the north coast and as far south in west Africa as Nigeria. In fact, Africa is normally seen as divided into two: the Islamic part, north of the Sahara desert, which still has links with the Arab world of the Middle East, and sub-Saharan or tropical Africa to the south. Islam added to the

richness of African culture, but the effect of some other intrusions was destructive. The worst intrusion of all was the European slave trade of the eighteenth century. Some eleven million Africans were torn from their native cultures and transported to the Americas.

A Sunday morning amateur soccer match, Kampala, Uganda

Masai women singing, Kenya

October 1995: Nelson Mandela, with a traditional weapon, greets supporters at an ANC rally.

European rule

In the late nineteenth century almost the whole of Africa became subject to European rule. European states—notably Great Britain, France, Germany, Belgium, and Portugal—seized parts of the continent, and in some areas, particularly in the south, white Europeans settled to farm. The European rulers did much to create the structure of modern Africa. They drew their own boundaries, setting up states in which different cultures and peoples found themselves strangely combined. They introduced their own languages, with the result that there are still English-speaking and French-speaking countries in Africa; they brought their own religion, Christianity.

Independence

In the 1960s the European powers began to leave and the independent states of modern Africa, still based on the European boundaries, appeared. The last of the African governments emerged in South Africa in 1994, when the white minority surrendered power to Nelson Mandela and his party, the African National Congress. Although Mandela had suffered many years of imprisonment for his belief in African majority rule, he was determined to forget the past and to build a new nation of South Africa shared by the black majority and the white minority. His attitude reminded the world that endurance and a sense of dignity are important values in African life.

Africans greeted their independence with jubilation. There were high hopes that the new African states

This house is in Mampong, Ghana. Today cocoa is one of Ghana's main foreign trade earners, second only to gold.

"Africa" by David Diop

David Diop's family came from Senegal, but he grew up in France. His poems (published in 1956) speak of ancient Africa, humiliated by colonialism but ready now to enjoy its freedom. Diop was killed in an air crash in 1960, aged 33.

Africa my Africa
Africa of proud warriors in ancestral savannahs
Africa of whom my grandmother sings
On the banks of the distant river
I have never known you
But your blood flows in my veins
Your beautiful black blood that irrigates the fields
The blood of your sweat
The sweat of your work
The work of your slavery
The slavery of your children
Africa tell me Africa
Is this you this back that is bent
This back that breaks under the weight of humiliation
This back trembling with red scars
And saying yes to the whip under the midday sun
But a grave voice answers me
Impetuous son that tree young and strong
That tree there
In splendid loneliness amidst white and faded flowers
That is Africa your Africa
That grows again patiently obstinately
And its fruit gradually acquire
The bitter taste of liberty.
(Moore and Beier, eds.,
Modern Poetry from Africa)

would develop fast, now freedom had come. In the 1960s and 1970s there was economic growth as education flourished and literacy and health care spread. Africa provided goods for the booming world economy: mainly minerals such as gold and copper, and cash crops such as coffee, tea, and cocoa.

Bronzes of a king and queen, from Ife, the religious capital of the Yoruba people

However, by the late 1980s and early 1990s the initial optimism had largely vanished. Despite some progress, Africa has remained steeped in poverty. Thirty of the forty poorest countries in the world are in the continent. One problem has been fast population growth. Traditionally, African families are large, with children helping on the family farm from an early age. But this can only make sense if there is a lot of spare land. By 1990 land resources were beginning to collapse under the weight of growing numbers. Years of drought saw the African deserts spreading farther into fertile land. There is little industry to replace agriculture, and there has never been enough money to provide good health care. Disease spreads easily. It is estimated that 60 percent of the world's deaths from AIDS in the year 2000 will be in Africa.

President Mobutu of Zaire—seen here with his wife, in December 1996—robbed his country of most of its wealth while he was in power from 1965 to 1997.

Then there are problems of government. The African political leaders who led their countries toward independence often had massive popular support. Few Africans wished the Europeans to stay. Once independence was won, however, it proved hard to create effective democratic governments in which ordinary people had a say. Sometimes a single tribe took control of a country. Often power was shared by a small elite who created a Western lifestyle for themselves. Dictators were common. President Sese Seko Mobutu of Zaire was one extreme example.

As governments lost popularity, they were challenged by those excluded from power, so Africa has known many civil wars, between rich and poor or between different peoples. The wars in Angola, Mozambique, the Sudan, and Ethiopia are just four examples. There was not only the horror of the violence but also the destruction of economies and, as a result, a mass of refugees seeking shelter in exile. Africa now has a larger proportion of its people as refugees than any other continent.

Taking responsibility

In 1992 the magazine *Ghana Drum* summed up the African political experience since independence:

"Some people will blame our colonial oppressors. Well in some cases part of it is true but a whole lot of the blame should be put squarely on our shoulders.... Independence was thought to be the beginning of the golden era where political freedom and expression, freedom of association, free enterprise, economic prosperity, responsibility and accountability of each and every one prevailed. These lofty ideals never happened because we replaced white imperialism with the black one." (Quoted in Ellis, ed., *Africa Now*)

All these problems were made worse by changes in international trade. The prices for many cash crops fell in the world markets, whereas the price of imported goods, such as oil, rose. Africa began to fall into debt. By 1990 Africa owed the rest of the world $180 billion, more than its entire output in a year. This has meant that aid has been essential—given not just through independent charities such as Oxfam, but through international organizations such as the International Monetary Fund and the World Bank. These have increasingly insisted that aid will be given only to governments that put their houses in order and rule democratically.

Soldiers in the civil war in Angola, with modern weapons supplied by international arms dealers

The mass of the people of Africa deserve a better future, one in which they can stand on their own feet and contribute to their own development and favored forms of government.

RWANDA: PRELUDE TO GENOCIDE

A traditional Tutsi dance

In 1994 the particular problems of Africa became focused in one of its smallest states, Rwanda. Rwanda is a fertile but overpopulated country, "a land of hills, huts, and banana groves," to the northeast of the giant central African state of Zaire (now renamed the Democratic Republic of Congo).

Belgian rule

From 1919 until its independence in 1962, Rwanda was a colony of Belgium. During this time, French became the language of administration and Catholicism the largest Christian denomination in the country.

Rwanda was home to three African peoples. The main two were the Tutsi, who made up 9 percent of the population, and the Hutu, who made up 90 percent. There were also the Twa, who made up only one percent of the population. It appears that the Tutsi, often

Stereotyped

The Belgians, who ruled Rwanda from 1919 to 1962, saw the Tutsi and the Hutu as entirely separate peoples, with the Tutsi the natural overlords of the Hutu. This view froze the two peoples into different roles and did much to create the hostility between them that followed independence. Here is the view of a Belgian administrator of the 1920s, Pierre Rykmans:

"The Tutsi were meant to reign. Their fine presence is in itself enough to give them a great prestige vis-a-vis the inferior races which surround them.... It is not surprising that those good Hutu, less intelligent, more simple, more spontaneous, more trusting, have let themselves be enslaved without ever daring to revolt." (Quoted in Prunier, *The Rwanda Crisis, History of a Genocide*)

The Rwandan countryside

Gerard Prunier, a French academic who has worked widely in Africa, described Rwanda before the genocide:

"Rwandese peasants are like large-scale gardeners and, apart from the remaining forested areas, the whole country looks like a gigantic garden, meticulously tended, almost manicured, resembling more the Indonesian or Filipino paddy fields than the loose extensive agricultural pattern of many African landscapes.... The first explorers who reached the Rwandese highlands after crossing the vast malarial and war-torn expanses of the Tanganyika bush felt that they were reaching a beehive of human activity and prosperity.... Every hill is dotted with dozens of settlements. Tutsi and Hutu, the notorious rival twins of Rwandese society, live side by side, on the same hilly slopes, in neighbouring settlements—for better or for worse, for intermarriage or for massacre...." (*The Rwanda Crisis, History of a Genocide*)

recognizable by their tallness, entered Rwanda some centuries ago and came to dominate the native Hutu. Traditionally, the Tutsi were cattle owners (cattle being the main source of wealth in Africa) whereas the Hutu remained peasant farmers. But the Tutsi and the Hutu came to speak the same language and share the same culture, and there has been some inter-marriage between the peoples.

Nevertheless, the Belgians believed that the Tutsi were the natural rulers of the country, and they preserved the Tutsi's status as overlords of the Hutu. In the 1930s they introduced identity cards for all Rwandans, and it was stated on these whether the person was Tutsi or Hutu.

Children in the countryside around Parc des Volcans, Rwanda

Rwanda in the 1960s

During Belgian rule Rwanda became one of the most strongly Christian countries in Africa. Looking back thirty years, Gerard Prunier describes the atmosphere and way of thinking in the country in the 1960s:

"Everything was carefully controlled, clean and in good order. The peasants were hard-working, clean-living, and suitably thankful to their social superiors and to the benevolent white foreigners who helped them. There was almost no crime, the few prostitutes were periodically rounded up for re-education and the church successfully opposed any attempts at birth control despite the fast growing population." (*The Rwanda Crisis, History of a Genocide*)

Independence

By the late 1950s it was clear that independence had to come for Rwanda, as for other African colonies ruled by Europeans. The only way that this could happen was for power to be transferred democratically—and this meant to the Hutu majority. The Hutu rejoiced at their opportunity to gain power, but the transfer took place with widespread attacks by Hutus on the Tutsi minority. Many Tutsis were forced to flee. A favored destination was the neighboring state of Burundi, which received independence at the same time but under a Tutsi-controlled government. Uganda was another popular choice and may have received 200,000 Tutsi refugees between 1959 and 1962, the year of full Rwandan independence.

July 1, 1962: The independence parade in the capital, Kigali. Children wave the new red, yellow, and green Rwandan flag.

Women at a meeting held by the United Nations in 1961, to prepare people for forthcoming elections. This would be the first time that women were able to vote.

In the years following independence, Rwanda appeared to be a well-run and stable country. It even made some economic progress, rising from third to nineteenth from the bottom in the world's poverty league. However, there was always discrimination against the Tutsi, and they were gradually eased out of every area of Rwandan life. Violence continued to be used against them.

In July 1973 there was a change of government when an army general, Juvenal Habyarimana, seized power. Habyarimana was from the north of Rwanda and, from this time on, northern Hutus were favored over those from the rest of the country. Habyarimana formed his own political party, the National Revolutionary Movement for Development (MRND), which came to dominate every area of life. Rwanda was one of the most tightly controlled countries in the world.

1961: A child of a Tutsi family, who fled Rwanda as power was transferred from the colonial government to a Hutu-controlled one

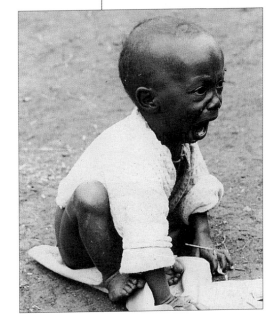

The Rwandese Patriotic Front

Meanwhile, the numbers of Tutsi in Uganda grew steadily, to about 700,000 by 1990. As Uganda experienced its own unrest, many of these people dreamed of returning to their homeland. In December 1987, discontented Tutsis, some of whom had picked up military skills while fighting in Uganda's civil wars, founded an army, the Rwandese Patriotic Front (RPF). It was dedicated to the return of the exiles to Rwanda, using force if necessary.

By the late 1980s Rwanda was beginning to be hit by the bad times experienced by the rest of Africa. The major underlying problem was population increase. The rate of growth was a staggering 3.2 percent per year, and this made Rwanda the most densely populated country in Africa, and second in the world only to Bangladesh. By 1992 an estimated 7.5 million people were crammed into 10,000 sq. mi. (26,000 sq. km), up to 750 people per square mile (400 per sq. km) of land.

There was also the collapse of world coffee prices in 1989. Some 75 percent of Rwanda's exports earnings came from the crop, so the collapse left the country with very little money to buy imports of oil and industrial goods that it could not produce itself. The economic crisis increased the tension among the Hutu, many of whom resented the powerful control of Habyarimana and his "northern" party.

Exercises at one of the Rwandese Patriotic Front training camps

As the country weakened, the RPF in Uganda sensed that this might be the moment to invade. On October 1, 1990, it launched an invasion of exiles (mainly Tutsi but with some Hutu exiles among them). The invading force was small, but it had the advantage of total surprise and made good progress before its commander was killed and it collapsed in confusion and defeat. A ceasefire was signed in March 1991, which allowed several hundred RPF soldiers to remain in Rwanda.

October 1990: After the defeat of the RPF, a member of the Zairean forces sent by President Mobutu to support President Habyarimana helps himself to loot.

Building up the Rwandan army

For Habyarimana, the defeated invasion provided a welcome excuse to strengthen his position. Being too poor to rebuild his government from within, he sought outside help; France proved ready to aid him.

Rwanda had not been a French colony. But France had kept strong links with French-speaking African countries, whatever their political background, and regarded it as important to keep a French influence in Africa. The French government had even supported the dictatorship of President Mobutu in Zaire, another former Belgian colony, through its worst excesses.

The Rwandan army was quickly built up. It expanded from 5,200 men in October 1990 to 50,000 by mid-1992. France supplied all the weapons needed and support for training, and the result was a well-disciplined force.

However, there was an ominous side to the buildup, of which the French may or may not have been aware. The new forces were increasingly used to round up the remaining Tutsis in Rwanda. President Habyarimana's own bodyguard seems to have become involved in selective killing of Tutsis and was aided in this by gangs of armed killers, the Interahamwe. Habyarimana may not have personally ordered the killings, but those close to him were certainly involved.

The early 1990s

In an interview with the organization African Rights, the Rwandan Minister of Finance, Marc Rugenera, explained his country's situation in the early 1990s:

"Those of us who were trying to run the country had serious problems to contend with. As Minister of Finance, my responsibility was the country's financial situation. And believe me, it was catastrophic. I knew the difficulties of paying salaries at the end of each month. I was aware of the famine which had ravaged parts of the country, the difficulties of maintaining the army and paying for the necessary imports. International donors had made continued assistance dependent on progress towards democracy...." (*Rwanda, Death, Despair and Defiance*)

International pressure

As his country's economic and political position worsened, Habyarimana came under increasing pressure to broaden his government so that other political parties, and the Tutsi themselves, could be included in power. The World Bank and the International Monetary Fund were threatening to make the giving of desperately needed aid dependent on the introduction of democracy. Habyarimana was trapped. He could not survive if he did not have aid, and so he signed an agreement, the Arusha Accords, in Tanzania in August 1993. He promised to move toward multiparty elections and to integrate the soldiers of the RPF into the Rwandan armed forces. The United Nations agreed to support the agreement by providing a task force of 2,500, the United Nations Assistance Mission to Rwanda (UNAMIR).

The death of Habyarimana

The move toward democracy outraged many of Habyarimana's supporters, especially those already organized into the Presidential Guard and the Interahamwe. They were terrified of the return of the Tutsi and other Hutus who supported a multiparty government. They started to spread violent anti-Tutsi propaganda, mainly through a newspaper called *Kangura* and through a radio station, Milles Collines.

The Hutu "Ten Commandments"

The following are extracts from the "Hutu Ten Commandments," which were circulated by extremist Hutu sources in 1990. The extremists were also strongly against any Hutu who formed relationships with Tutsis.

"1. Every Hutu should know that Tutsi woman...works for the interest of her Tutsi ethnic group...we shall consider a traitor any Hutu who
—marries a Tutsi woman
—befriends a Tutsi woman
—employs a Tutsi woman as a secretary.
4. Every Hutu should know that every Tutsi is dishonest in business. His only aim is the supremacy of his ethnic group. As a result any Hutu who does the following is a traitor
—makes a partnership with Tutsi in business
—invests his money or the government's money in a Tutsi enterprise
—lends or borrows money from a Tutsi.
5. All strategic positions, political, administrative, economic, military and security should be entrusted to Hutu.
8. The Hutu should stop having mercy on the Tutsi."
(*Kangura*, December 1990)

Anti-Tutsi propaganda

This notice was seen on the border between Rwanda and Zaire in April 1992. (The Bantu was the name generally used for the native African peoples of southern Africa, to distinguish them from outsiders, both white and black.)

"Attention Zaireans and Bantu people! The Tutsi assassins are out to exterminate us. For centuries the ungrateful and unmerciful Tutsi have used their powers, daughters and corruption to subject the Bantu. But we know the Tutsi, that race of vipers, drinkers of untrue blood. We will never allow them to fulfil their dreams...." (Quoted in Crawford, "Hutus see France as their saviour," *Financial Times*, June 27, 1994)

The Tutsi were denounced as outsiders, "cockroaches," who were only interested in coming back to Rwanda as overlords.

When President Habyarimana was forced to sign a second agreement in Tanzania in April 1994, promising to integrate Tutsis in his government, the Interahamwe made up their mind to get rid of him. As soon as they had attacked his plane and he was dead, they were ready to carry out their plans.

Weapons used in the genocide

The Interahamwe

A Rwandan newspaper, *Umuranga Mubangutsi*, reported in March 1992:

"The Interahamwe are trained military killers. It has been said in many quarters that the MRND government is training Interahamwe in commando tactics such as the use of knives, machetes, rope trapping and binding of victims and silent guns so as to kill people. Training places are Gishwati [a forest area] in Gisenyi, Rukari in Nyanza, Commune Bicumbi, and in the Mount Kigali forest." (Quoted in African Rights, *Rwanda, Death, Despair and Defiance*)

GENOCIDE

The assassination of President Habyarimana on April 6, 1994, unleashed one of the most horrifying events of modern world history: a massacre of the Tutsi people of Rwanda, in which perhaps as many as a million died in the space of a hundred days.

Nzabakirana, who survived the massacres, has drawn some of the horrors that he saw. Children like this were traumatized by the torture and killings they witnessed. A United Nations report explained that these children's trauma was expressed in "sadness, insomnia, nightmares, a permanent fear of being killed, mistrust of those around them, and depression."

Because one human group was the target and because of the effective and brutal way in which the killings were carried out, the massacre was seen as an act of genocide—a term that refers to the attempted extermination of a people simply on account of their national, racial, or religious background.

The UN defines genocide

This is the definition of genocide given in Article II of the United Nations Convention for the Prevention and Punishment of the Crime of Genocide (1948):

"Genocide includes any of the following acts committed with intent to destroy, in whole or in part, a national, ethnical, racial or religious group as such:
a. killing members of the group;
b. causing serious bodily or mental harm to members of the group;
c. deliberately inflicting on the group conditions of life calculated to bring about its physical destruction in whole or in part;
d. imposing measures intended to prevent births within the group;
e. forcibly transferring children of the group to another group."

The Holocaust

The best-known example of genocide in the twentieth century is a European one: the so-called Holocaust, the attempted extermination of the Jews of Europe by the Nazi government during World War II (1939–45). Some six million Jews were rounded up and transported across Europe to special camps where they were put to death by gassing or shooting. It was only as troops of the Allied armies reached the camps, during their reconquest of Europe in 1945, that the true scale of the Holocaust was revealed.

The impact on world opinion was immense. The revulsion was such that, when the United Nations was established at the end of the war, it drew up a special Convention on Genocide, in the hope of preventing such a tragedy ever happening again. Members of the United Nations who signed the convention promised to work together to prevent genocide and to punish anyone found guilty of involvement in genocide, wherever he or she had fled to. Rwanda itself signed the convention. Sadly, it was not enough to prevent the events that followed Habyarimana's death.

Planning genocide

In order to exterminate a people, there needs to be effective planning. Victims must be identified, separated from others, rounded up or arrested, and killed. The Holocaust again provides an example. The Nazi Party had made no secret of its anti-Semitism (hostility toward Jews). After it came to power in Germany in 1933, it began to mark out and discriminate against German Jews, isolating them through propaganda and by boycotting Jewish businesses and the services of Jewish doctors and lawyers, for example. The Jews were easy to segregate, as many already lived in their own communities, the ghettos. The mass killing of Jews began in the 1940s and was organized by the SS, the Nazi death squads. As the Nazis conquered Europe in the 1940s, Jewish communities across the continent who came under their rule were eliminated.

There needed to be similar planning for the extermination of the Tutsi, and it was clear that this was in hand before the death of President Habyarimana. Propaganda had already been used to spread fear and hatred of the Tutsi. Now, exaggerated reports of a Tutsi attack, backed by the RPF, were broadcast on the radio and Hutus were told to defend themselves. "Take your spears, clubs, guns, swords, stones, everything—hack them, those enemies, those cockroaches, those enemies of democracy," ran one broadcast.

These two sisters were hacked on the neck with machetes and left for dead, but a week later they were rescued by their father.

As tension rose, government forces and the Interahamwe used the administrative structure to pass down orders from Kigali, the capital, to the countryside. Within a few days, local burgomasters (government officers) throughout Rwanda were putting in hand the killing of Tutsis in their area. These people could be identified easily through the official files that the burgomasters kept, but most Hutus knew exactly who among their neighbors were Tutsi.

Involving local Hutus

There was a clear policy of involving local Hutus in the massacres. Peasant farmer Jean Bosco Bugingo explained how this was done:

"The burgomasters were spreading the rumour that the Tutsis in our area had had a meeting and were planning to kill the Hutus. The stories were brought by soldiers...they went to the local officials and asked them to spread the information to the councillors and to the local people....
Our councillor, Joseph Munyaneza, told the Hutus to rise up and defend ourselves....

"The councillors called a meeting...at the meeting they said Hutus must kill Tutsis and everybody who was against the government, so that when the RPF came they would not have anyone to rule. Many Hutus pointed out that they had lived with and intermarried with these people they are being told to kill. Munyaneza said: 'Either you kill them or you will be killed.' He told us that we would be moving around with soldiers and that they would see to it that either you killed or you died....
They said that people should come to the councillor's office to collect machetes and other weapons." (African Rights, *Rwanda, Death, Despair and Defiance*)

The massacres

Eyewitness accounts of the horrific events of the next three months make difficult and harrowing reading. Local officials, aided by the Interahamwe, aroused local Hutus into a frenzy of fear and hatred of the Tutsi. The Tutsi, they were told, were about to rise up against them. Only a complete elimination of the Tutsi, including children and babies, would rid Rwanda of the threat they posed. Meetings were held where weapons were handed out and the where-abouts of prominent Tutsis were made public. All Hutus were urged to join the Interahamwe in carrying out the extermination. Those, and there were many, who refused to join in the mass hysteria, were threatened themselves with death. It was as if all Hutus were being forced by their leaders to take a shared responsibility for the killings. The killings were systematic and thorough.

Whole villages were wiped out.

 ## Systematic killing

Gloriose Mukakanimba was interviewed at a health center, where she had come for medical help for machete cuts. She had been a teacher and lived at Gatare. Her husband and her brother had been killed in the massacres, and she had no news of her three children, from whom she had become separated. She told the interviewers:

"After the President's death, the Presidential Guard began to kill Tutsis. They began what they call their 'work' on Thursday morning. At first, the target was prominent and rich men. But on Saturday, soldiers and Interahamwe began to attack ordinary people. They shot you just because you were Tutsi. When they started to use machetes they didn't even bother to ask for ID cards. It was as if they had carried out a census; they knew you were a Tutsi. On Sunday they started house-to-house killings in our area. It was systematic; soldiers told the Interahamwe to ensure that there were no survivors. As our fear intensified, people abandoned their homes to hide in bushes and wherever they could." (African Rights, *Rwanda, Death, Despair and Defiance*)

An attack on a church

Justin Kanamugire, a thirty-two-year-old Tutsi peasant farmer, was one of the few who survived. He described what happened:

"Our sector was attacked on the night of the 10th [April]. We watched as our houses were burned down and our cows stolen and eaten.... As we were fleeing towards the Adventist church of Muhomboli, some of the villagers threatened us. They said we were deluding ourselves because there was no border around the church which could prevent them from penetrating the church....

"On the 13th, we saw an enormous group of militia from the sector of Butembo and neighbouring sectors. They surrounded the church....

Before the genocide the church could comfortably accommodate about a thousand people. But during the genocide it was packed. There were at least two thousand refugees. We had to put the benches aside to create space for people.

"It was the 13th that the Interahamwe decided to attack us, at about midday. They threw grenades through the windows and doors which they managed to break down. Once they overcame all resistance from the refugees, they entered inside the church. I saw that death was waiting for me. I pretended to be dead and listened to the movement of the killers as I lay underneath numerous corpses. They withdrew at about 6 pm. At midnight I left the church, which was overflowing with corpses...." (African Rights, *Rwanda, Death, Despair and Defiance*)

Outside a church east of Kigali, at the end of May 1994

Word soon got round the Tutsi community of what was in store for them and they fled to wherever they could hope for protection, often to their local churches or to hospitals. But there was no safe shelter from armed troops and a Hutu population worked up into hysteria.

In fact, it proved very easy to isolate Tutsis in these meeting places and kill them without mercy.

A camp of people who had escaped the massacres

Hutu help

Not all Hutus were involved in the killings, and some even helped Tutsis to escape, as Claude Kanamugire explains here. He had already been wounded with a spear.

"When the killing started on the Friday, I ran to one of the meeting rooms [of the local church] and hid in the ceiling. After a while, I became so weak with hunger that I went back home to look for something to eat. When I got there I realized I had no house to go to because it had been razed to the ground. I went to see an old Hutu woman I knew. She hid me in her house, looking after me as best she could. After a while, some neighbors discovered I was there. Afraid they would come back to look for me, she took me to a coffee field, covering me up with leaves. I stayed there for some time and left on the 18th [April]. I went to Nyakabingo, to the home of an old Hutu friend of my father's. He took me to a bush which was far from his home. I stayed there for two months. The old man used to bring me food." (African Rights, *Rwanda, Death, Despair and Defiance*)

The Tutsi, despite all rumors of an uprising, had almost nothing with which to defend themselves and were easily dealt with. The Interahamwe would return day after day to finish off the wounded or loot the bodies and pursue any survivors into the bush. Survivors had an indescribable time. Often wounded themselves, they had to shelter under the dead bodies of their relatives for days until it was safe to come out. The impact of their wounds, the loss of their families, and the horrific sights they had seen left deep and irremovable scars for most of them.

The sole survivor of a village massacre

The scenes that greeted later observers were horrific: piles of corpses, many of them hacked to death with machetes and rooms full of bodies into which grenades had been thrown until no one was left alive. Where before there had been the lively chatter of African village life, there was now a dreadful silence. Tutsi homes had been looted and their simple possessions lay scattered all around the villages. Because the Tutsi were regarded as immigrants, many were killed alongside rivers, and their bodies were sent floating out of the country. This provided the first evidence to the outside world of the horror of what was happening.

THE REFUGEES

As the massacres began, a provisional government was set up in Kigali, the Rwandan capital. Although it included some opposition politicians, it was still dominated by members of Habyarimana's party, the MRND. It proved completely unable to stop the escalating violence. Now forces of the Rwandese Patriotic Front (RPF) still in Uganda went into action. They crossed into Rwanda and headed for Kigali, hoping to rescue the 600 RPF soldiers who had remained there after the ceasefire of 1991.

June 1994: RPF soldiers push forward into Rwanda.

After encountering resistance from government troops in Kigali, the RPF began to spread through the rest of Rwanda. There was little opposition to them. They certainly caused casualties and probably carried out some atrocities of their own as they advanced—but nothing on the scale of the genocide whose aftermath they now discovered.

On the move out of Rwanda, 1994

As the RPF advanced, the Hutu began to panic. They knew that the RPF would exact some kind of revenge, either through the law or through revenge killings. In many cases, the burgomasters who had overseen the massacres now took the initiative in gathering local populations and marching them toward the Rwandan borders.

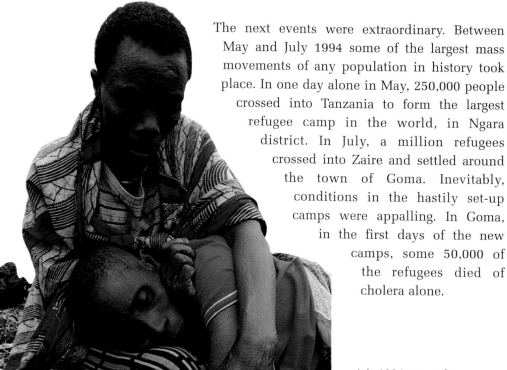

The next events were extraordinary. Between May and July 1994 some of the largest mass movements of any population in history took place. In one day alone in May, 250,000 people crossed into Tanzania to form the largest refugee camp in the world, in Ngara district. In July, a million refugees crossed into Zaire and settled around the town of Goma. Inevitably, conditions in the hastily set-up camps were appalling. In Goma, in the first days of the new camps, some 50,000 of the refugees died of cholera alone.

July 1994: at a refugee camp 6 mi. (10 km) north of Goma, a man comforts his wife who is dying of cholera.

Forced to flee

Mamerita Uwamariya, a 30-year-old teacher from Kibuye, described how people were pressured to leave Rwanda:

"By the end of June there were all sorts of fresh meetings telling everyone to go to Zaire. The burgomaster was telling people that anyone related to him had to go, but people were angry, telling the burgomaster: 'First you tell us to kill people. Now you are telling us to leave. If you couldn't carry out your plans, why did you implicate so many innocent people?'....
People were given a deadline by which they must be in Zaire. We were told that whoever did not leave by the deadline would be swept away by the Interahamwe who would come from behind. The prefet [another government official] was moving around with a loudspeaker, urging people to flee toward Zaire. Soldiers were shooting in the air, making people stampede at an even greater rate towards the border...."
(Quoted in African Rights, *Death, Despair and Defiance*)

Providing aid

The full horror of the suffering was beamed into the world's homes through television, and the response was immediate. International aid organizations such as the British-based Oxfam and the International Red Cross were soon hurrying aid toward Rwanda and the camps that now surrounded the shattered country. It is estimated that some 150 different international charities responded to the Rwandan crisis.

The sheer scale of the refugee crisis is shown in this view of one of the camps around Goma.

In one two-day period, 14,000 refugees died in Goma. Aid agencies had to transport the dead in trucks and bulldoze them into mass graves.

A deserted country

After the genocide of the Tutsi and the exodus of the Hutu, many areas of Rwanda were left empty. BBC journalist Fergal Keane described crossing from Uganda into Rwanda in the summer of 1994, after the massacres:

"A few months ago the road [from Uganda into Rwanda] had literally hummed and vibrated with the traffic of several nations. On the day we arrived it was empty. Nothing moved or breathed anywhere that we could see. The only traffic now was relief trucks and whatever the RPF was rolling down to Kigali.... The rains had brought forth a great tangle of vegetation. With nobody to cultivate the fields the weeds and wild grasses were sweeping across the countryside. In less than five minutes we had gone from a country [Uganda] where people were going out into the fields, gathering wood, cooking food, walking and enjoying the new morning, to a place where nothing stirred. Only the breeze rising occasionally to flatten the rampant grasses and the steady growl of our diesel engines interrupted the silence. It was as if a giant Hoover had been directed down from the heavens and sucked away everything that moved."
(*Season of Blood, A Rwandan Journey*)

In recent years the professionalism of aid charities had improved enormously, but the problems of dealing with this crisis in central Africa were formidable. Aid had to be organized quickly in order to save lives in an area where there were few proper roads and no administrative framework. It was also important to channel aid where it was most needed, and to make sure that it was not siphoned off by those who did not need it. It became clear in the Rwandan crisis that, while a great deal of aid reached the refugee camps outside Rwanda, some areas of southern Rwanda where conditions were equally desperate

A truck crew works to make a road passable.

received little aid at all. There were problems of coordination among the many different organizations, and it became obvious that some of the smaller organizations, despite their undoubted commitment, simply did not have the experience of African conditions to be effective.

Goma, July 1994: An International Red Cross worker pours out rice—aid that thousands of refugees received.

To aid or to blame?

In addition to all these problems, the refugee camps in Zaire presented the aid organizations with a major dilemma. The camps were run by the very leaders who had organized the exodus from Rwanda, and many of these leaders had been behind the genocide. A large number of the refugees had themselves been killers. Should they receive any help? Many aid organizations felt that it was their duty to provide humanitarian aid to all who needed it, whether or not they had committed crimes. They were supported by world opinion, as people saw on their television screens only the desperate plight of the refugees and not the evidence of the dreadful acts carried out by many among them in the weeks before.

Leaders in the camps

The leaders were described in a UN report:

"Former soldiers and militiamen have total control of the camps...they have decided to stop, by force if necessary, any return of the refugees to Rwanda...it now looks as if these elements are preparing an armed invasion of Rwanda and that they are both stockpiling and selling food aid distributed by charities in order to prepare for this invasion."
(*Africa News Report*, November 28, 1994)

Providing aid

Maurice Herson of Oxfam's Emergency Department explained:

"You must have heard the accusation that we (Oxfam, the aid world in general) have been supporting the killers from Rwanda.... We all could—in theory—have stopped providing water and food and shelter and other services to the two million other refugees in Zaire and Tanzania, and many many more people would have died. That would have been hard to justify to ourselves and to others.... When the forces that now run Rwanda took over, a million people fled the country. Oxfam called on the UN to fulfil its mandate and separate those guilty of mass murder from the many others who were either guilty of lesser crimes or not guilty at all.... Legally, those guilty of acts of genocide are not entitled to be considered as refugees with the rights of protection and care which go with that status.... This was not done, and the aid agencies went on...serving both genuine refugees and the others." (*Oxfam Campaigner*, Spring 1997)

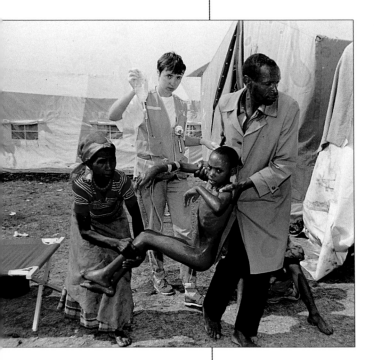

A French doctor takes care of a refugee child in Goma, August 1994.

On the other hand, some people held that the crime of genocide was so appalling that all aid should be withheld from those associated with it. They argued that a military force should enter the camps to sort out those who could be accused of the genocide from those who were innocent. This argument was strengthened by evidence from the refugee camps that the suspected leaders were taking the aid and often using it to maintain their own power in the camps. Former members of the Interahamwe were receiving the best of what was available. There was even evidence that Hutu extremists were being rearmed in the camps so that they could return to Rwanda by force.

However, the camps were given humanitarian aid through the United Nations relief organizations and other aid agencies, and the death rates from disease dropped to normal levels.

A lighter side of bringing aid

 ## Gacumbitsi is king

Fergal Keane described the refugee camp at Benaco in June 1994:

"It is not the aid agencies or the United Nations or the Tanzanian government who are in control here. No, this vast city of huts and tents is the province of the Hutu warlords. Gacumbitsi [a former burgomaster whom eyewitnesses had seen organizing killings] is king here. He could have us beaten up, thrown out, even killed. But he is too clever for that. That might force the agencies or the Tanzanians to act as if they did have some control, and that would interfere with the system of power and patronage he has managed to transplant successfully from Rwanda to Benaco. Instead he has decided to tolerate us, humor us. He might suffer the indignity of being questioned and accused but he knows what everybody knows. Nobody is going to come into his stronghold and take him away." (*Season of Blood, A Rwandan Journey*)

Laurent Kabila coordinated the overthrow of President Mobutu in 1996–97 and became the new leader of Zaire.

Civil war in Zaire

The power of the Hutu killers in the camps was actually supported by President Mobutu of Zaire. Mobutu met several of their leaders and made no secret of his desire for a Hutu government back in Rwanda. But Mobutu was about to face his own challenge. His rule of Zaire since 1965 had been appallingly corrupt, and he had reduced his large and rich country to poverty. In October 1996, civil war broke out in Zaire when Laurent Kabila led a number of anti-Mobutu groups against the government. Among Kabila's supporters were Tutsi refugees in Zaire.

Mobutu's regime had long since lost any respect or support. Now it began to collapse, and soon Kabila found himself in charge of the whole of eastern Zaire. With his backing from the Tutsi, he had no time for the Hutu, and the latter knew their time was up. In October 1996, in another extraordinary mass movement, some 720,000 Hutu refugees started walking back from their refugee camps to Rwanda. A further 400,000, apparently including many of the worst killers who knew they could never return to Rwanda, fled from Kabila's forces deep into the African bush. Little was heard of them, though their situation was clearly desperate. In March 1997 the United Nations set up a special mission to try to send these refugees, particularly the children among them, back to Rwanda. Many must have perished alone and been abandoned in the forests.

Refugees on the road back from Zaire to Rwanda

RWANDA AND THE INTERNATIONAL COMMUNITY

During the summer of 1994, the RPF gained control of most of Rwanda, and in July it set up a Government of National Unity. Although this new government included some politicians from outside the RPF (the president and prime minister were Hutu) and declared that it was above tribalism, it was inevitably associated with the Tutsi. The government's authority in a country where the majority of the population was still Hutu was bound to be weak.

Above: The chairman of the RPF, Alexis Kanyarengwe, a Tutsi, became vice-president in the new Government of National Unity.

An RPF soldier on guard in Kigali, July 1994

Furthermore, the problems facing the new government were daunting. There were vast human tragedies to deal with: the aftermath of the genocide and the mass movement of refugees both inside and outside the country. The economy was shattered. Much of the countryside had been abandoned. There was a need for international support on a far greater scale than could possibly be provided by the aid agencies. How could the international community help?

Boutros Boutros-Ghali was Secretary-General of the UN, 1992–96. In 1993 he was welcomed at a relief center in Mogadishu, Somalia.

The United Nations

The United Nations might be an organization that could offer hope. Not only did it claim to represent the international community as a whole, rather than the interests of individual member states, but it also had a range of agencies concerned with international human rights and individuals in distress. The United Nations High Commission for Refugees (UNHCR) was one. The United Nations had a special interest in enforcing its Convention on Genocide.

The United Nations also had long experience of providing peacekeeping forces. UN peacekeeping forces are forces made up of soldiers from member states of the United Nations, which work under direct control of the United Nations in particular trouble spots. In certain instances, peacekeeping forces have been very effective: in monitoring elections, for instance, or in maintaining disputed borders, such as that between the Turks and the Greeks in Cyprus or between North and South Korea.

Mogadishu, Somalia, June 1993: A Pakistani UN soldier watches over Somalis who had been captured for having guns.

The aftermath in Rwanda

In the autumn of 1994, the Secretary-General of the United Nations reported to the General Assembly on emergency assistance to Rwanda:

"Para 15. The war and massacres have wreaked havoc on every aspect of life in Rwanda. The whole structure of government collapsed and in the post 6th April turmoil government offices were completely looted and personnel displaced. The health system, already strained by high infant mortality, high fertility rates and the AIDS epidemic, has been completely destroyed. Access to safe drinking water has decreased...as traditional spring water sources were damaged and contaminated and pipe distribution systems were seriously damaged. The entire system of education has been paralysed with schools standing empty or destroyed.

Para.16. Agricultural and pastoral activities have been severely disrupted. Crops planted in February already badly affected by poor rainfall should have been harvested in July. Reports show that most fields were abandoned....

Para. 18. Damage to agricultural production and infrastructure represents the most visible consequence of the crisis along with thousands of wounded Rwandans and countless amputees. It has inflicted incalculable mental and emotional suffering. It has been estimated that in large parts of the country every individual has lost a family member and/or had home or possessions destroyed. The psychological trauma of these events will leave debilitating scars for years to come."
(*The United Nations and Rwanda, 1993–96*)

Peacekeeping forces might also be used to distribute food or to protect civilians in war zones. However, peacekeeping forces face particular problems in war zones. Can peacekeepers actually use force themselves, to protect civilians against attack, for instance? Do they not then risk, as one more group using violence, becoming part of the problem they were sent to solve? This dilemma was faced by UN peacekeeping forces in the African state of Somalia, who became directly involved in the civil war there, and by peacekeeping forces in Bosnia, who were accused of failing to protect civilians.

UNAMIR

The United Nations had already been involved with Rwanda through the United Nations Assistance Mission to Rwanda, UNAMIR, set up in 1993. This was a force of 2,500 men sent to oversee the transition to multiparty democracy and the integration of RPF soldiers into the Rwandan army.

The forces were still in Rwanda when the 1994 genocide began. Indeed, one of the first events of the genocide was the brutal killing of ten Belgian soldiers from the force, who were guarding the prime minister. The governments providing the UN troops then began to panic and, on April 21, a decision was made to withdraw all but 270 men of the force.

An appeal to keep UNAMIR at full strength

On April 21, 1994, the Secretary-General of the Organization of African Unity, Dr. Salim Salim, wrote to the Secretary-General of the UN:

"It would be a tragic wrong that at a time when African leaders and the Organization of African Unity are intensifying their efforts in support of those of the United Nations to end the conflict in Rwanda, an impression should be created of reluctance, to say nothing of outright withdrawal, on the part of the United Nations from Rwanda. Such a position of the UN will certainly be a tremendous let-down to the people of Rwanda, who look up to the international organization with great hope and expectation."(Quoted in *The United Nations and Rwanda, 1993–96*)

It was true that the UNAMIR troops were vulnerable but, at the same time, the withdrawal appeared to signal to the international community—and, in particular, to Africans—that the United Nations did not care about what was happening.

As the full horror of the genocide became apparent, the UN tried to build up a new peacekeeping force. It was agreed in the summer of 1994 to send 5,500 troops to

The failure of the UN

The Secretary-General of the UN, Boutros-Ghali, tried but failed to raise another peacekeeping force for Rwanda. On May 31, 1994 he said:

"We must all recognize that we have failed in our response to the agony of Rwanda and thus have acquiesced in the continued loss of human life. Our readiness and our capacity for action has been demonstrated to be inadequate at least and deplorable at worst, owing to an absence of collective political will."

Rwanda, and yet this new force was never raised. With support from the United States, it might have been possible. But the United States had provided a large part of the force to Somalia and had been horrified by the problems it had faced there. It would give no help for the Rwandan force. It was not until late August 1994 that a smaller UN force did arrive in Rwanda.

UN forces from the UK arrive in Kigali, August 1994.

Speaking out against the UN

Jean Paul Biramvu, a survivor of the massacres and a human rights activist, remarked:

"We wonder what UNAMIR was doing in Rwanda. They could not even lift a finger to intervene and prevent the deaths of ten of thousands of innocent people who were being killed under their very noses....
An institution must have the capacity to be effective. But the UN protects no one. They had been sent to Kigali to assure the security of Kigali. How can they protect the security of Kigali when they are doing nothing to protect its people?" (Quoted in African Rights, *Rwanda, Death, Despair and Defiance*)

Cheers as French troops arrive in Rwanda.

The French step in

One nation did, however, come forward to help: France. The French had been involved in Rwanda before, in support of President Habyarimana. They now declared that, for humanitarian reasons, they would send in a task force to offer the Rwandans

Too late?

A group of Rwandan (Tutsi) Catholic priests told Cardinal Roger Etchegaray, president of the Papal Council for Justice and Peace:

"We consider the French military intervention, describing itself as a humanitarian one, is cynical. We note with bitterness that France did not react during the two months when the genocide was being committed, though she was better informed than others. She did not utter a word about the massacres of opposition members. She did not exert the slightest pressure on the self-proclaimed Kigali government, although she had the means to do so. For us, the French have come too late for nothing...." (From the BBC Summary of World Broadcasts for July 11, 1994)

protection. There were many who doubted the sincerity of the French government. Some said that it was using the genocide as an excuse for maintaining France's influence in central Africa, and that it had only acted after President Nelson Mandela of South Africa had suggested sending African troops to help. And, after all, had not France helped build up many of the forces that had carried out the genocide?

Nevertheless, the United Nations, its own attempts to raise a peacekeeping force unsuccessful, gave support to the French operation and "Operation Turquoise" went ahead. It involved 2,500 soldiers occupying an area in southwest Rwanda (with a population of about 1.5 million) between late June and mid-August 1994, and offering some protection for refugees there.

Injured Rwandans are airlifted to safety.

However, it seems that many of the Hutu killers were among those sheltered by the French, and there was no attempt to isolate them and bring them to justice. When the force was withdrawn, the Rwandans were left with no long-term protection.

August 1994: carrying a bag of cereal given out by humanitarian organizations. Despite the publicity given to Africa's problems, international aid remains a tiny proportion of the rich world's spending.

Ideas for the future

The Rwandan crisis, combined with the experience of Bosnia and Somalia, raised many concerns about sending peacekeeping forces to areas of war. Yet such areas and the civilians in them cannot simply be abandoned. An urgent task for the international community is to sort out how forces can be raised and trained to help effectively in this kind of crisis. Regional organizations, in this case the Organization of African Unity (OAU), also have a role to play.

Relief agencies appreciate the help of the United Nations particularly in organizing and in coordinating their work. Working together ensures that these agencies do not duplicate each other's efforts or concentrate them in the wrong areas. The agencies may also need help to deal with the governments involved in a crisis and may need armed protection in some cases—for instance, when taking food through a war zone. A United Nations presence can provide all these kinds of support.

In many cases of disaster United Nations agencies now play prominent roles in coordinating aid. But there needs to be a far greater commitment from the international community, particularly when an expensive military force is required to provide the ordered background without which relief work cannot take place. Lack of commitment has proved to be the major stumbling block in the past. It does seem that the international community failed the civilians in Rwanda, as it did those in Bosnia in the Yugoslav civil war, at their time of need.

RECONCILIATION AND JUSTICE

From the autumn of 1994, some form of order was restored to Rwanda. Schools began reopening, and fields were cultivated once more. But the wounds left by the genocide were deep. Reconciliation was not made any easier by the return of perhaps some 800,000 Tutsi exiles from abroad. In many cases these people took land that had been abandoned by Hutus, so there was the possibility of further tensions as refugee Hutus returned. Attempts by the new government to break up refugee camps within Rwanda, in the hopes of forcing their inhabitants home, often ended in bloodshed.

A young Hutu, April 1995

"The fire inside"

A woman survivor of one of the massacres spoke of her feelings:

"I want vengeance. I want revenge. I am hurting so much inside....
So much death, so much grief, so many families wiped out, and we are
to forget about it? The fire is out, at least here in Kabuga, but not the fear.
And what about the fire inside each of us?
   "When I was first evacuated, it was such a thrill to see people you could
not be sure were still alive. But our discussions are so sad—so and so is
dead, this one did not make it, of that family no one is left.... No, I don't
feel like talking to anyone. I don't have space in my heart for more sorrow,
more sadness. This is why, for me, I must leave Rwanda for some time.
Maybe if I can rest my mind in a more peaceful country for a while,
this desire for vengeance will diminish...." (Quoted in African Rights,
Rwanda, Death, Despair and Defiance)

Hutu extremists

A journalist, Robert Block, worried that the Hutu extremists would never understand their responsibility for the massacre:

"Perhaps most disheartening of all is that most of the Hutus still do not recognize that what happened to the Tutsis was a crime of enormous proportions. There is a state of collective denial by almost everyone you meet in the camps. People do not see their ordeal as self-imposed but as the fault of the Tutsis and the RPF: 'We are dying here because of the Tutsis and the cockroaches of the RPF who want to rule over us,' said one woman, who was absolutely convinced of the correctness of killing Tutsis." (*The Independent on Sunday*, July 31, 1994)

Reconciliation does not mean forgiveness. One starting point for reconciliation, however, is the effective punishment of those who organized the genocide. Arresting the leaders and condemning them publicly after a fair trial offered the only way of dealing with the desire for revenge and putting an end to the waves of killing and counter-killing that have scarred Rwandan society.

Trials in Rwanda

Within Rwanda, the killers could, of course, be charged under normal domestic law (as well as under the United Nations Convention on Genocide, which was part of that law). But there needed to be a respected and well-organized legal system to make sure that the process was carried out fairly. The Rwandan government set up courts, and gradually those suspected of organizing the killings were gathered into overcrowded prisons to await trial. (Kigali prison, designed for 1,500 prisoners, eventually held 5,000.)

Froduald Karamira (left) at the opening of his trial in Rwanda, January 1996. He was accused of being a leader of those who carried out the genocide.

In August 1996 a law was passed, classifying the killers according to their level of involvement. Organizers of the genocide would be liable to the death penalty.

The problems of dealing with the accused were immense. The authority of the new government was weak, and it had few courts or judges. It was extremely difficult to find out who was responsible for organizing the killings, particularly when so many Hutus were involved, and there were few innocent victims left alive. It was clear from the beginning that the Rwandan courts would find it difficult to work fairly, and progress is slow. When the first trials began, there was widespread concern about possible unfairness, voiced for instance by the human rights organization Amnesty International. Nevertheless, by February 1997, thirteen death penalties had been passed.

Many of those in the Rwandan prisons were teenagers who had been caught up in the killings.

Demand for justice

Frederic Mutagwera, a Rwandan lawyer, explains why he believes it is so important to punish those who organized the killings:

"Massacres have taken place in Rwanda as far back as 1959 and the early sixties. Nothing has ever been done about them. No one is ever punished ...it is precisely because there has not been the political will to punish them that the next round of killings invariably begins....
No one is suggesting that every peasant who took a machete should be punished. But those who organized the peasants, who told them to hunt Tutsis and Hutus of the political opposition—the local government officials, the soldiers, the politicians—they must be judged, tried, and punished. It is not the severity of the punishment that is important, but the certainty that actions have consequences." (Quoted in African Rights, *Rwanda, Death, Despair and Defiance*)

Crimes against humanity

There is another way of bringing to justice those guilty of such crimes as genocide: through an international tribunal. The punishment of "crimes against humanity" has its origins in the Nuremberg Trials, which were held at the end of World War II. The victors of the war, Great Britain, the United States, and the Soviet Union, felt that the horrific nature of Nazi rule, the extermination of Jews and others, and the launching of the war itself were such appalling crimes against humanity that the main Nazi leaders should be tried and punished.

Nazi war criminals on trial in Nuremberg, 1945

There were worries that the victors were hardly the best people to judge those they had defeated, and that they might be making up new forms of crime, "crimes against humanity," after they had been committed. However, there was general approval of what the Nuremberg Trials achieved. A reasonably fair trial was possible because there was ample evidence of the Holocaust from documents, films, and the extermination camps themselves, and the main Nazi leaders were easily identifiable.

After this, the United Nations, set up after World War II, attempted to define certain crimes that should be punished by the international community. Genocide is one, punishable through the UN Convention on Genocide, which came into force in 1951. Another kind is war crimes (the massacre of unarmed civilians, for instance), which are punishable through the Geneva Conventions of 1949.

It was only very recently that the first war crimes tribunal was set up, in fact. This was in the Hague, Netherlands, to deal with "criminals" from the conflict in former Yugoslavia. In May 1997, a Bosnian Serb, Dusan Tadic, was the first man to be convicted by the international tribunal, for "persecution" and complicity in murders. However, he was only one of just eight people who had actually been arrested, out of seventy-four suspected war criminals, and his trial showed the enormous difficulty of getting fair evidence from the chaos of a civil war.

Crimes of genocide

In November 1994 the United Nations set up an international tribunal to prosecute those responsible for genocide in Rwanda. The statute of the tribunal was framed in almost identical terms to that of the tribunal set up to try war crimes in Yugoslavia. The two tribunals were also linked by having common officials.

"Article 3. The International Tribunal for Rwanda shall have the power to prosecute persons responsible for the following crimes when committed as part of an independent or systematic attack against a civilian population on national, political, ethnic, racial or religious grounds
    (a) murder
    (b) extermination
    (c) enslavement
    (d) deportation
    (e) imprisonment
    (f) torture
    (g) rape
    (h) persecution on political, racial and religious grounds
    (i) other inhumane acts."
(From Security Council Resolution S/RES/955, November 8, 1994)

Georges Rutaganda, accused of genocide and crimes against humanity, was the first Rwandan to be charged by the UN tribunal. He pleaded not guilty.

The UN tribunal on Rwanda

The United Nations set up an international tribunal to deal with genocide in Rwanda, in November 1994. The tribunal was to sit in Arusha, in neighboring Tanzania. It had few resources. Even in November, there were only four investigators working in the whole of Rwanda. As more joined them, it was clear that most were inexperienced and had problems in communicating in local languages. It proved difficult for the UN tribunal, as it had done for the Rwandan

Giving up hope

As time passed and the trials in Rwanda and Arusha moved slowly, some survivors began to give up hope:

"It is as if nobody cares. Two years appears to be a long enough time for the government leaders to forget abut the corpses that littered our land, churches, schools, everywhere.... It makes me wonder how people can fail to read the signs of the times. The very people, I mean those who perpetrated genocide, are not repentant. Yet some politicians are even talking about reconciliation and even blanket amnesty." ("A survivor" quoted by Ndahiro Tom in *Tribunal*, September/October 1996)

Hope for the future

A Rwandan priest told an interviewer

"If out of all this there emerges a decent government of national unity, where law is established and implemented in a fair manner, then the process of reconciliation can begin. But that will not in itself mend the thousands of broken hearts in Rwanda. There are just too many wounded hearts in our country. Even with the right political climate it will take a long, long time for these hearts to heal. That must be accepted. There can be no rush. If there is, there will be no way out." (Quoted in African Rights, *Rwanda, Death, Despair and Defiance*)

courts, to gather accurate information over which those accused could be brought to justice. It was not until January 1997 that the first UN trials began.

With so long a delay between the crimes and the punishment, the danger is that the world community will simply forget the genocide. Also, unpunished crimes encourage more of the same, and in Rwanda, where the tradition of revenge killing has become so deep-rooted, that is a particularly serious matter.

These two young Rwandans drew their hopes for the future. Nzigihima dreamed of cars, to help his mobility. Mukamponga drew a handshake: an internationally recognized symbol of agreement and peace.

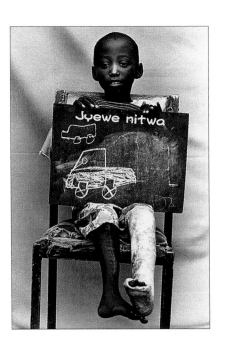

CONCLUSION

The trauma caused by what happened in Rwanda in 1994 will take a long time to heal. Although there are many Hutus and Tutsis who wish to bridge the gap between the two peoples and move on to a new future, there are also many for whom hurt remains at such a deep level that, for the moment, any reconciliation is impossible. That is why public condemnation of the killers through the courts is so important.

There are also more than memories to hold up progress. Tutsi exiles moved into deserted Rwandan countryside. As Hutu refugees have returned home and found them, there have been new disputes over land. Underlying these disputes is the problem of the continuing high rate of population increase. Tensions caused by this increase were surely one of the factors leading to the intensity of the 1994 killings. The future of Rwanda remains unsure.

An African response

In a speech in June 1994 at a meeting of the Organization of African Unity in Tunis, the South African president, Nelson Mandela, said:

"Rwanda stands out as a stern and severe rebuke to us all for having failed to address the interdependence of human rights, stability, peace, democracy and development.... We know it as a matter of fact that we must have it in ourselves as Africans to change all this. We must, in action, assert our will to do so."

Yet life in Africa moves on. In May 1997 President Mobutu of Zaire was finally driven into exile. Little is known of his successor, Laurent Kabila, but he offers at least the possibility that Zaire, renamed by Kabila the Democratic Republic of Congo, will see a period of stability in which its wealth is used for its people and not just for its rulers. Congo has immense mineral

"The African Renaissance"

President Nelson Mandela spoke on the fall of Mobutu's regime in Zaire, in May 1997:

"I am convinced that our region and our continent have set out along the new road of lasting peace, democracy, social and economic development. The time has come for Africa to take full responsibility for her woes, to use the immense collective wisdom she possesses to make a reality of the ideal of the African Renaissance whose time has come."

resources and their exploitation would benefit not only Congo but also the countries surrounding it. One hope for Rwanda is that surplus population could be attracted outside the country, as migrant labor.

There is another hope. As Mobutu's Zaire collapsed, President Nelson Mandela of South Africa offered to help ensure a peaceful transition of power from Mobutu to Kabila. It was a sign that one of Africa's strongest countries was prepared to take some wider responsibility for its continent. This is encouraging. The only way for Africa to provide healthy prospects for its people is for the continent to take responsibility for its own future.

May 4, 1997: Nelson Mandela chairs a meeting between President Mobutu of Zaire (left) and his successor, Laurent Kabila (right).

CONN LIBRARY
Wayne State College
1111 Main Street
Wayne, NE 68787

African values

Blaine Harden is a journalist, who was the *Washington Post*'s chief correspondent in sub-Saharan Africa in the late 1960s. He wrote:

"Though continuously battered, African values endure. They are the primary reason why, beyond the sum of Africa's dismal statistics and behind two-dimensional images of victims (a frightened mother with a dead baby and disintegrating fingertips), the continent is not a hopeless or even sad place. It is a land where the bonds of family keep old people from feeling useless and guarantee that no child is an orphan, where religion is more about joy than guilt, where when you ask a man for directions he will get in your car and ride with you to your destination—and insist on walking home.

"The Africans themselves are the only way to make sense of the grim news out of Africa. More than any people on earth, their future is in jeopardy and they deserve our attention. It is premature, I think, to pass final judgment on their experiment. Scrawled on the tailgates of exhaust-belching trucks that rumble through the back roads of West Africa is a grassroots warning to those inclined to write the continent off. It says: 'No condition is permanent.'" (*Africa, Dispatches from a Fragile Continent*)

Opposite: A Rwandan mother with her baby, born as she traveled out of the country in 1994.

This does not mean that the international community should desert Africa. Africa forms part of humanity. It is the birthplace, in fact, of the modern human race, and it deserves to be seen as more than just a provider of goods for European supermarkets or a recipient of aid. It is the responsibility of the international community to be aware of the African plight, to understand what can be done to help Africans make their own way, and, above all, to be willing to provide expertise and support when they are asked for.

In truth, the response of the international community, including the United Nations, in 1994 meant that the genocide in Rwanda was as much an international failure as an African one. It has many lessons for us all.

DATE LIST

1919
Belgium takes over Rwanda from its former colonial ruler, Germany. The Tutsi minority is confirmed as a ruling class.

1926
The Belgians introduce identity cards stating ethnic identity. (The cards are made compulsory in 1933.)

1959
As independence comes closer, Hutus rise up against the Tutsi. Many Tutsis flee to neighboring countries.

1962
Rwanda gains independence from Belgium under a Hutu government. Many more Tutsis flee to Uganda.

1973
Juvenal Habyarimana, a Hutu from the north of Rwanda, becomes president. He sets up a one-party state. The party is the National Revolutionary Movement for Development (MRND). The Tutsi face further discrimination.

1987
Exiled Tutsis in Uganda set up the Rwandese Patriotic Front (RPF).

1989
Growing economic distress in Rwanda after world prices for coffee collapse.

1990 October
The RPF launches an invasion of Rwanda.

1991
A cease-fire is called, but RPF troops remain in Rwanda. President Habyarimana builds up the Rwandan army, with French support. The Interahamwe are trained as a Hutu fighting force.

1993
At Arusha, Tanzania, President Habyarimana agrees to share power with other parties and to join the RPF with the Rwandan army. A United Nations force, UNAMIR, is sent to oversee the moves toward power-sharing. However, Habyarimana does little, and there is growing propaganda from Hutu extremists against the RPF and the Tutsi. These extremists are increasingly fearful that Habyarimana will surrender Hutu supremacy.

1994 April
In Dar es-Salaam, Tanzania, Habyarimana makes a second agreement to share power. As he returns to Rwanda on April 6, his plane is shot down by Hutu extremists. Massacres of Hutu opposition leaders and of Tutsis begin in the Rwandan capital, Kigali, and spread to the rest of the country.

April 21
Most of the UNAMIR troops are withdrawn by the UN.

1994 April-May	Genocide of the Tutsi is now well under way. RPF troops move through Rwanda in an attempt to stop the killings. The Hutu flee before them. Vast refugee camps are formed in Zaire and Tanzania.	**1996 August**	Rwandan law classifies those involved in the killings according to the seriousness of their crimes. By February 1997, Rwandan law courts have sentenced to death 13 organizers of the genocide.
June	The United Nations authorizes France to send its own force into Rwanda, in "Operation Turquoise." French troops arrive in late June and stay until August. A smaller UN force arrives in August.	**October**	Civil war in Zaire drives most Hutu refugees back into Rwanda. Other refugees flee further into the Zairean bush. In March 1997, the United Nations launches an operation to return them to Rwanda.
July	A Government of National Unity is formed in Kigali by the RPF. It contains some Hutu members.	**1997 January**	UN tribunal begins hearing cases of war crimes and genocide.
November	The United Nations sets up a tribunal in Tanzania to judge those who have been involved in the genocide.	**May**	The collapse of the government of President Mobutu in Zaire. Laurent Kabila takes power, with the support of South Africa.

RESOURCES

Two books introducing the Rwandan tragedy are:

Vassall-Adams, Guy. *Rwanda: An Agenda for International Action.* Oxfam Insight, 1994.

Waller, David. *Rwanda: Which Way Now?*, 2nd ed. Oxfam, 1996.

For advanced study of the genocide:

Rwanda, Death, Despair and Defiance, compiled and published by African Rights, London, 2nd ed., 1995 (the fullest account, with eye-witness stories)

McCullum, Hugh. *The Angels Have Left Us: The Rwandan Tragedy and the Churches.* Geneva: World Council of Churches, 1995 (another eyewitness account)

For background to the genocide:

Destexhe, Alain. *Rwanda and Genocide in the Twentieth Century.* New York: New York University Press, 1995.

Keane, Fergal. *Season of Blood, A Rwandan Journey.* New York: Viking Penguin, 1996. (an accessible journalist's account)

Prunier, Gerard. *The Rwanda Crisis, History of a Genocide.* New York: Columbia University Press., 1995. (demanding reading)

On peacekeeping issues:

Making Peace. Teaching about Conflict and Reconciliation, Oxfam, 1997 (a resources pack)

Edmund Cairns, *A Safer Future: Reducing the Human Cost of War*, Oxfam, 1997 (contains material on international tribunals)

GLOSSARY

burgomasters officials responsible for overseeing local government in Rwanda.

cash crops crops, such as coffee, grown for selling overseas.

domestic law the laws in force within a particular state.

ethnic identity an identity based on membership of one race or culture—such as Hutu or Tutsi in Rwanda.

extremist a person who holds very strong political views in support of which he or she may even be ready to kill.

genocide the extermination of a particular ethnic group.

Holocaust the attempted extermination of the Jews during World War II.

Interahamwe "they who stand together." Groups of Hutu extremists trained to spread hatred and violence against the Tutsi.

international law laws that a number of nations agree they will enforce. For instance, the United Nations law against genocide.

International Monetary Fund (IMF) organization set up in 1944 to ensure international financial stability.

International Tribunal a law court set up to enforce international law.

machete a broad knife that can be used in farming or as a weapon.

MRND the National Revolutionary Movement for Development— the political party that ruled Rwanda from 1973 to 1994.

Nuremberg Trials trials at which the German Nazi leaders were tried for war crimes and genocide.

Operation Turquoise military operation in which French troops maintained order in part of southern Rwanda, June–August 1994.

peacekeeping force a force, often raised by the United Nations that tries to keep the peace between warring groups.

propaganda information that is created or deliberately exaggerated in order to spread hatred.

Rwandese Patriotic Front (RPF) a political group, mainly of Tutsis, founded in Uganda in 1987. It was prepared to fight to overthrow the Rwandan government of President Habyarimana. The RPF dominated the Government of National Unity set up in Rwanda in July 1994.

United Nations (UN) international organization set up in 1945 to improve cooperation among nations in the cause of peace.

United Nations Assistance Mission to Rwanda (UNAMIR) a UN force of 2,500 soldiers sent to Rwanda in 1993 to oversee power-sharing between the Hutu government and its opponents.

United Nations High Commission for Refugees (UNHCR) organization set up by the United Nations to oversee the care and resettlement of refugees.

war crime a major crime committed during a war: for instance, the deliberate killing of civilians.

World Bank a bank set up in 1944, focusing on international aid and development.

INDEX

aid **5, 15, 22, 35, 36, 37, 38, 39, 41, 48, 58**
AIDS **14, 43**
Amnesty International **51**
arms dealers **15**
army, Rwandan **21, 23, 44**
Arusha Accords **4, 23**

Belgium **6, 12, 16, 17, 18, 44**
Bosnia **43, 48, 53**
Boutros-Ghali, Boutros **42, 43, 45**
burgomasters **28, 33, 34, 39**
Burundi **4, 18**

cash crops **13, 15, 20**
cholera **34**
Christianity **12, 16, 18**
civil war **14, 43**
civilizations, African **10, 13**
coffee **13, 20**
colonies, European **12, 13, 14, 18**
Congo, Democratic Republic of **16** (*see also* Zaire)
copper **13**

debt **15**
deserts **8, 14**
Diop, David **13**

France **12, 21, 22, 46, 47**

genocide **25, 26, 27**
(*see also* UN Convention on Genocide)
Germany **12**
gold **12, 13**
Goma **34, 35, 37**
Great Britain **12**

Habyarimana, Juvenal, President **4, 5, 19, 20, 21, 22, 24**
Holocaust **26, 27, 52**
human race **10, 58**
Hutus **4, 16, 17, 18, 19, 20, 23, 28, 29, 30, 31, 33, 38, 39, 40, 41, 47, 49, 50, 51, 56**

identity cards **5, 17**
independence:
   African **12, 13, 14, 15**
   Rwandan **18, 19**
Interahamwe **5, 22, 23, 24, 28, 29, 32, 38**
International Monetary Fund **5, 15, 22**
Islam **10, 11**

Kabila, Laurent **40, 56, 57**

Mandela, Nelson **12, 47, 56, 57**
Mobutu, Sese Seko President of Zaire **14, 21, 40, 56, 57**

MRND, *see* National Revolutionary Movement for Development

National Revolutionary Movement for Development (MRND) **19**
news (TV and press) **9, 35, 37**
Ntaryamisa, President of Burundi **4**
Nuremberg Trials **52**

oil **15, 20**
Operation Turquoise **47**
Organization of African Unity (OAU) **44, 48, 56**

population increase **14, 20, 57**
Portugal **12**
poverty in Africa **14, 19**
Presidential guard **5, 22, 23**
prisons, Rwandan **50, 51**
propaganda **23, 24, 27**

refugees **14, 18, 34, 35, 37, 38, 40, 47, 49, 56**
Rugenera, Marc **22**
Rwandese Patriotic Front (RPF) **20, 21, 23, 27, 33, 41, 44**

Salim Salim, Dr. **44**

slave trade **11**

Somalia **43, 45, 48**

South Africa **12, 57**

Tanzania **4, 24, 34,**

trials

in Rwandan courts **50,**
51

international **52, 53**

Tutsi **4, 16, 17, 18, 19,**
20, 22, 23, 27, 28, 30,
31, 32, 40, 41, 49, 50,
56

Twa **16**

Uganda **18, 20, 32**

United Nations **23, 26, 39,**
40, 42, 43, 47, 48, 52, 58

Convention on Genocide
26, 42, 50, 53

Geneva Conventions **53**

peacekeeping forces **42,**
43, 44, 45, 47, 48

UNAMIR **23, 44, 45**

UNHCR **42**

war crimes tribunal **53,**
54, 55

United States **45**

Uwilingiyamana, Agatha,
Rwandan prime minister
6, 44

weapons **4, 15, 21, 24, 29**

World Bank **5, 15, 22**

Zaire (Democratic Republic
of Congo) **14, 16, 24, 34,**
37, 40, 56, 57

© Copyright 1998 Wayland
(Publishers) Ltd.

SOURCES

The following were used as sources of information for this book:

African Rights. *Rwanda, Death, Despair and Defiance.* 2nd edition. London, 1995.

Chernoff, John. *African Rhythm and African Sensibility.* Chicago: University of Chicago Press, 1981.

Ellis, Stephen, ed. *Africa Now.* Portsmouth, NH: Heinemann, 1996.

Harden, Blaine. *Africa: Dispatches from a Fragile Continent.* New York: HarperCollins, 1991.

Keane, Fergal. *Season of Blood: A Rwandan Journey.* New York: Viking Penguin, 1996.

Martin, Phyllis and Patrick O'Meara, eds. *Africa.* 3rd edition. Bloomington, IN: University of Indiana Press, 1995.

Moore, G. and U. Beier, eds. *Modern Poetry from Africa.* New York: Penguin, 1963.

Prunier, Gerard. *The Rwanda Crisis, History of a Genocide.* New York: Columbia University Press, 1995.

The United Nations and Rwanda, 1993–96 (UN report)